Snap books®

Justin Timberlake

by Jen Jones

CAPSTONE PRESS
a capstone imprint

Snap Books are published by Capstone Press,
151 Good Counsel Drive, P.O. Box 669, Mankato, Minnesota 56002.
www.capstonepress.com

092009
005618CGS10

 Books published by Capstone Press are manufactured with paper
containing at least 10 percent post-consumer waste.

Library of Congress Cataloging-in-Publication Data
Jones, Jen.
    Justin Timberlake / by Jen Jones.
    p. cm. — (Snap books. Star biographies)
    Includes bibliographical references and index.
    Summary: "Describes the life and career of Justin Timberlake" — Provided by publisher.
    ISBN 978-1-4296-3399-4 (library binding)
    1. Timberlake, Justin, 1981- 2. Singers — United States — Biography. I. Title. II. Series.
ML420.T537J66 2010
782.42164092 — dc22
[B]   2009036380

Editor: Jennifer Besel
Designer: Ashlee Suker
Media Researcher: Marcie Spence
Production Specialist: Laura Manthe

Essential content terms are **bold** and are defined at the bottom of the page where they first appear.

Table of Contents

CHAPTER 1

Hitting a High Note

Perched behind a piano and dressed in a sporty white blazer and hip T-shirt, Justin Timberlake was on top of the world. It was February 8, 2004, the night of the 46th Annual Grammy Awards. Justin had just rocked a high-energy performance of his hit "Señorita." Legendary trumpeter Arturo Sandoval and a jazz band had accompanied him in the performance.

Yet all of that couldn't compare to the two Grammys he'd won earlier that night. For years, Justin had traveled the world and sang to sold-out arenas. He had millions of fans. But until that night, he had never nabbed the famous statue. Justin's first solo album, *Justified*, changed all of that. At the Grammy Awards, he scored a win for best pop vocal album for *Justified*. He also won best male pop vocal performance for his song "Cry Me a River."

After receiving two Grammys, Justin was pumped as he performed at the awards show.

Justin considered winning a Grammy a huge success in his career.

The Los Angeles Staples Center was packed with the world's most successful musicians. And Justin was counted among them. The star-studded affair included Madonna, Beyoncé, Christina Aguilera, and Martina McBride. Norah Jones, John Mayer, Alicia Keys, and the Black Eyed Peas graced the stage. Justin even received a few encouraging words from Sting backstage. Cheering Justin on was Lynn Harless, his mother, who had supported his career from the start. There was no doubt about it. Justin had finally arrived!

By taking home top honors that night, Justin proved he could make it on his own. Today JT, as fans call him, is a musical superstar with more than 17 million solo records sold. But achieving his dream didn't come without some hard work.

"This is officially the greatest moment of my life." — Justin in his acceptance speech at the 2004 Grammy Awards.

He's Got the Look

Justin doesn't have to be on the red carpet to look like a million dollars. Over the years, the singer has developed his own sense of style. While with *NSYNC, Justin often sported baggy, colorful athletic clothes. Those clothes fit with the style of the 1990s and the band's peppy attitude. Yet when JT broke out as a solo artist, his fashion sense followed "suit." Now you'll find Justin wearing sleek suits, tailored sweaters, and anything that fits his effortlessly cool image.

Justin's hair has also changed quite a lot over the years. Justin's hair is naturally curly, a feature he hates! So he's tried quite a few styles to find one he likes. From super curly to mega blond, his hair has received almost as much attention as his music. And fans aren't shy about their thoughts on his hairstyles. In fact, fans still talk about how much they hated the cornrows he wore in 2000.

Fans usually love Justin's style. But few people were sad when he got rid of the cornrows.

The Prince of Pop

The year 1981 was an amazing time for pop music. MTV first hit the airwaves. It also marked the birth of Justin Randall Timberlake. Born on January 31 in Memphis, Tennessee, Justin entered the world ready-made for stardom. Memphis is known as the home of soul music. And both of his parents were extremely musical. His mom, Lynn, played several instruments. His dad, Randy, was a talented bluegrass singer.

Though young Justin's voice was in perfect harmony, his home life was not. Lynn and Randy divorced when Justin was just 3 years old. Two years later, Lynn married Paul Harless. Along with Lynn, Paul supported Justin's dream to become a singer. Justin's father, Randy, also married again and had two more sons, Jonathan and Stephen. Randy supported his son but wasn't quite as involved in Justin's climb to stardom.

Justin's mom, Lynn Harless, now runs a company that manages entertainers. She named the company Just-In Time Entertainment, after her son.

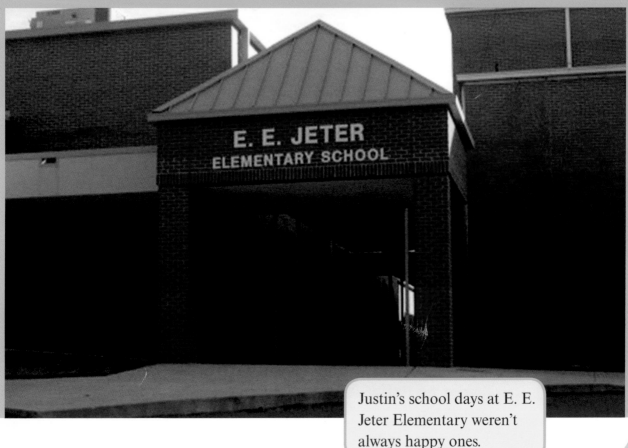

Justin's school days at E. E. Jeter Elementary weren't always happy ones.

Not so Popular

Growing up in the Memphis suburb of Shelby Forest, Justin wasn't as popular as he is today. While attending E. E. Jeter Elementary, Justin was teased for having mega-curly hair and acne. Kids called him mean names like pizza face and Brillo Pad. To stay happy, Justin focused on the two things he loved most — sports and singing.

Along with playing basketball at school, Justin took vocal and piano lessons. Under vocal teacher Bob Westbrook's direction, Justin learned techniques for proper breathing, stage presence, and pitch. He also got valuable performance experience as one of the Bob Westbrook Singers.

As his talent grew, Justin dreamed of becoming famous. In 1992, he got his first taste of the limelight. At 11 years old, Justin performed on the TV show *Star Search*. Using his middle name as his stage name, Justin Randall hit the stage in full cowboy gear. He sang Alan Jackson's country song "Love's Got a Hold on You." Justin didn't win, but that didn't keep him from working toward success.

Justin got his first taste of fame when he competed on *Star Search*.

Becoming a Mouseketeer

It turned out luck would soon be on Justin's side. He'd been thinking about trying out for the Disney TV show *The All New Mickey Mouse Club*. To support his dream, Lynn and Justin moved to Orlando, Florida, while Paul stayed in Tennessee. At Justin's **audition**, he sang "When a Man Loves a Woman." The casting directors were wowed by his performance. Soon Justin became the newest addition to the *MMC* cast.

Life on the *MMC* set was a big change for Justin. The show filmed five days a week, and the days were packed. Justin had to be on set by 7:00 each morning.

Justin (back center) met future girlfriend Britney Spears (front center) on the set of *MMC*.

audition — a tryout performance for a performer

The cast had on-set tutoring for three hours. Afternoons were spent in rehearsals, makeup, and **wardrobe**. Then they taped the live show for a studio audience. Of course, the show wasn't all work and no play. Spending so much time together made the cast very close. They had a lot of fun working on the silly skits and high-energy songs.

Yet all good things come to an end. *The All New Mickey Mouse Club* ended in 1995. Justin worried that his singing career was over. He had no idea that he would soon be on a wild ride to superstardom.

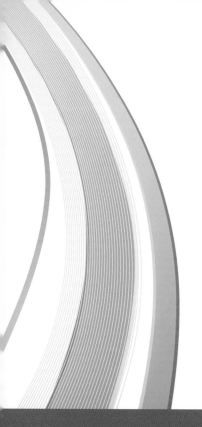

The Star-Making Machine

Justin wasn't the only one who became a huge star after appearing on *MMC*. The show was a gold mine for new talent. Castmates Ryan Gosling and Keri Russell both went on to become respected actors. Ryan was up for an Oscar for his movie *Half Nelson*. Keri starred in the popular TV show *Felicity*. Christina Aguilera and Britney Spears were also Justin's castmates. JC Chasez, JT's *NSYNC band mate, starred in the Disney show too. An exclusive club indeed!

wardrobe — the place where clothing used on a TV show is kept

CHAPTER 3

Working in Harmony

After *MMC*, Justin and Lynn moved back to Tennessee. Justin tried to get a record deal on his own. But it seemed that no opportunities were coming his way. Later in 1995, singer Chris Kirkpatrick approached both Justin and his former castmate JC Chasez. Chris wanted to form a band much like the successful Backstreet Boys. Already onboard was Joey Fatone, who was well-known in music circles. Both Justin and JC signed on. Completing the group was Jason Galasso, who was soon replaced by Lance Bass.

As a brand-new group, the five were excited to start making music. But first they needed a name. Justin's mom stepped in to save the day. Lynn's idea was to use the last letter of each member's first name. She also wanted to give a shout-out to the guys' amazing harmonies. The result? *NSYNC!

Justin and Lance Bass (back) with Chris Kirkpatrick, JC Chasez, Joey Fatone (front left to right), created the powerhouse band *NSYNC.

The Fab Five

Lynn **managed** the group for a brief time. Then in 1996, the group signed with manager Lou Pearlman. Pearlman also managed the Backstreet Boys. Pearlman set the boys and Justin's mom up in a house in Orlando. The house became the group's headquarters. There they took singing lessons, worked on dance routines, and rehearsed. Justin also did schoolwork with a tutor there. The house became known as "the compound."

Soon Pearlman arranged an audition for the group with some executives at the recording label BMG. From that meeting, *NSYNC scored a record deal with BMG's division in Germany. Stardom was in sight.

*NSYNC went on to become international teen idols. Yet the boy band didn't reach star status without years of hard work. The group started touring Europe. While on tour, the band also recorded its self-titled **debut** album. In its first week of sales, the album reached number one in Germany. The first single, "I Want You Back," hit the German Top 10. More success followed in other European countries. The boys returned to the states in 1998 to try their luck at home.

"I thought I was the coolest guy. Nobody could tell me anything or I'd be like, 'I have a record contract!'"
— Justin in an interview with *Rolling Stone*.

manage — to take care of a band's schedule, performances, and transportation

debut — a first of something

Justin (second from left) and the guys put on huge performances for fans.

In the United States, the fab five's popularity exploded! In just one year, *NSYNC went 10 times **platinum** with four number-one Billboard singles. The band followed its first album with *Home for Christmas*, a collection of holiday tunes. Then in March 2000, the band released its third album, *No Strings Attached*. Fans snapped up 1 million copies of that album in one day! A 2001 *Rolling Stone* cover called the heartthrobs the "biggest band in the world."

But the fourth and final *NSYNC album, *Celebrity*, set the stage for Justin's solo career. On this album, Justin took on **producing** and songwriting duties. Though *NSYNC was at the height of fame, Justin was itching to do something different.

platinum — when more than 1 million copies of an album are sold
produce — to be in charge of putting together an album

Going Solo

In 2002, *NSYNC members went their separate ways to explore new opportunities. JT spent the beginning of the year working with the industry's hottest producers.

The result was *Justified*, an album that gave Justin a whole new sound. Gone were the peppy pop tunes. In their place were smoother, more sophisticated R&B jams. But one thing that didn't change was Justin's relationship with his mom. Lynn supported him in his new solo career.

The album's release was a huge hit. Fans everywhere were buzzing about JT's new songs, especially "Cry Me a River." Justin also teamed up with former Mouseketeer Christina Aguilera for a concert tour.

Justin used his dance skills when he performed on his *Justified* tour.

CHAPTER 4

A Talented Heartthrob

After all the **hype** surrounding *Justified*, Justin decided it was time for a long-overdue break. After all, he'd been touring, making music, and promoting albums nonstop for more than five years. In 2004, Justin took time off from music. He began to explore some of his other talents.

Fame in Film

Justin wanted to explore an acting career. He starred in a Disney TV movie called *Model Behavior* in 2000. But Justin felt it was time for more adult roles. During 2007, he starred in three movies — *Black Snake Moan*, *Alpha Dog*, and *Southland Tales*. He also put his famous voice to good use as Artie in *Shrek the Third*. Though many critics doubted Justin's acting ability at first, he soon won them over.

hype — big claims made about something in order to promote it

Justin's fun, goofy personality came out as he worked on *Shrek the Third*.

Justin's acting talent is well-known today. In 2008, *Entertainment Weekly* named him one of its top 30 actors under age 30. In August 2009, he hit the big screen again in *The Open Road*. In the film, Justin starred opposite Jeff Bridges. Justin played the son of a famous athlete who travels cross-country with his father.

Funny Guy

Justin is known for his sense of humor. So it's no surprise that he has included plenty of comedy roles in his acting career. As a frequent guest on *Saturday Night Live*, Justin has been front and center for some of the show's most outrageous moments. He has even won two Emmy awards for his awesome job performing on the show! He also showed off his silly side in 2008's *Love Guru*.

"The reason I got into film is because I needed something inspiring, but more intimate, that I didn't have to do in front of 18,000 people every night."
— Justin in an interview with *Rolling Stone*.

Justin (left) and Jimmy Fallon (right) got down and got a little silly in a skit for *Saturday Night Live*.

Justin uses his good looks to promote his clothing line, William Rast.

Fun In Fashion

Justin also explored new talents beyond music and acting. Since 2005, Justin and best friend Trace Ayala have been turning heads with their clothing line. The high-end line is named William Rast — a combination of their grandfathers' names. And what better way to sell the clothes than to have Justin show them off? He often performs at fashion shows and models the clothes in online videos for the brand.

Along with making people look good, Justin wants to help them smell good. In 2009, he partnered with Givenchy to endorse the men's fragrance Play. The fragrance comes in a bottle designed to look like an MP3 player. Justin is featured in many of the product's advertisements.

Soul Food

When he's not working, Justin enjoys dining in his restaurants. Justin owns two restaurants in New York City, Destino and Southern Hospitality. Serving the foods of southern Italy, Destino attracts many celeb customers. Southern Hospitality is inspired by Justin's Tennessee roots. Besides southern comfort food and tasty BBQ, visitors also enjoy live musical entertainment.

CHAPTER 5

Life Offstage

Life in the spotlight doesn't provide much privacy. **Paparazzi** go wherever JT goes. They push and shove to get the latest picture of the A-lister. That's why Justin doesn't go anywhere without his bodyguards.

But fame has its perks too. As of 2008, Justin was worth about $44 million. With that money, he's been able to keep up with his shoe collection. He owns a pair of almost every Nike Air Jordan shoes ever made. Justin also enjoys collecting cars. He has six cars, including a Dodge Viper and a Porsche 911. He also has six Harley Davidson motorcycles in his garage.

Heartbreaker

Justin has dated many of Hollywood's leading ladies. His most well-known relationship was with Britney Spears. They'd known each other since their *MMC* days, but they didn't admit to being a couple until 2000. As the prince and princess of pop, it seemed fitting that Britney and Justin would fall in love.

paparazzi — aggressive photographers

Justin's romance with Jessica Biel made front-page headlines.

The pair mysteriously broke up in 2002. Rumors flew that JT's song "Cry Me a River" was written about Brit! Justin has also had relationships with A-list actresses Cameron Diaz and Jessica Biel.

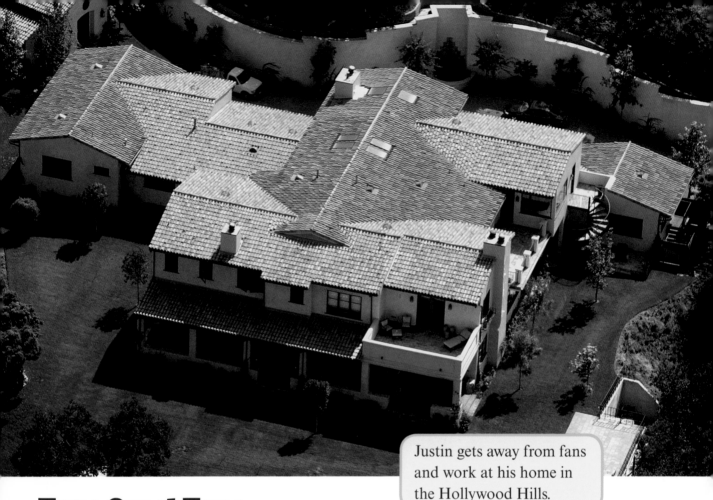

Justin gets away from fans and work at his home in the Hollywood Hills.

Home Sweet Home

When he made it big with *NSYNC, Justin bought a new house in Orlando for about $1 million. He took great pride in decorating it, creating a country kitchen and a safari-themed bedroom. A white grand piano formed the centerpiece of his all-white living room. The game room featured a tropical theme. In 2006, he sold this home for $2 million.

Now Justin relaxes in his sweet bachelor pad in the Hollywood Hills, California. This $8 million home has five bedrooms and eight bathrooms. His four dogs keep him busy whenever he's at home. He has two boxers named Buckley and Brennan. He also has a pit bull/lab mix and another dog named Billy.

Lots of Heart

Justin has a lot of money, but he also has a lot of heart. In 2001, he started the Justin Timberlake Foundation. The charity's goal is to provide money for music programs in public schools. The first grant went to E. E. Jeter Elementary, Justin's grade school in Tennessee.

Justin also does a lot of work for the Shriners Hospitals for Children. He hosted PGA golf tournaments to raise money for the hospitals. In late 2008, JT released a new single as a fund-raiser for the Shriners Hospitals. He also gathered a bunch of his famous friends for charity concerts to benefit the hospitals. Alicia Keys, Taylor Swift, and Ciara were among the performers at the 2009 event called "Justin Timberlake and Friends."

"This is about an opportunity that every person should enjoy, no matter what career they aspire to. I want to do everything I can to make sure other people can benefit from music education."

— Justin speaking about his foundation in an interview with *Time for Kids*.

Justin produced Esmée's first album. He also cowrote several of her songs.

A Golden Talent

Music has been and will always be a central part of Justin's career. In 2006, he released his second solo album. The album hit number one on the charts and was nominated for four Grammy awards. He nabbed two of the golden statues for best dance recording and best rap/sung collaboration.

Justin has also found a home writing and producing songs for stars like Madonna, Ciara, Beyoncé, 50 Cent, Rihanna, and T.I. In addition, Justin has a great eye for new talent. He started his own record label called Tennman Records. Recently he worked with and signed Esmée Denters. Justin discovered Esmée on YouTube.

Don't forget to look for Justin in a theater near you. In 2010, he will reprise his role as Artie in *Shrek Forever After*. He's also working as music supervisor for the film *The Devil and the Deep Blue Sea*.

Mega-Star

Justin seems to have done it all — from acting to fashion design to restaurant ownership. Over the years, he's wanted to be like everyone from Michael Jordan to Michael Jackson. But these days, it's pretty good just to be Justin Timberlake.

Justin's brilliant smile and his incredible talent are a winning combination. He's a star known all around the world.

Glossary

audition (aw-DISH-uhn) — a tryout performance for an actor or a singer

debut (DAY-byoo) — a first showing

hype (HIPE) — exaggerated claims made about something in order to promote it

manage (MAN-ij) — to be in charge of a band, taking care of scheduling, transportation, and other things

paparazzi (pah-puh-RAHT-see) — aggressive photographers who take pictures of celebrities for sale to magazines or newspapers

platinum (PLAT-uhn-uhm) — selling more than 1 million copies of an album

produce (pruh-DOOSS) — to be in charge of putting together an album, a movie, or a TV program

wardrobe (WARD-robe) — a place containing a collection of clothing used on the set of a movie or TV show

Read More

Cefrey, Holly. *Justin Timberlake.* Contemporary Musicians and Their Music. New York: Rosen, 2009.

De Medeiros, James. *Justin Timberlake.* Remarkable People. New York: Weigl, 2009.

Napoli, Tony. *Justin Timberlake: Breakout Music Superstar.* Hot Celebrity Biographies. Berkeley Heights, N.J.: Enslow, 2009.

Internet Sites

FactHound offers a safe, fun way to find Internet sites related to this book. All of the sites on FactHound have been researched by our staff.

Here's all you do:

Visit *www.facthound.com*

FactHound will fetch the best sites for you!

Index